Anyway, Don't Be a Stranger

A Collection of Poetry & Prose

Written by Syed Haider

This is a work of creative nonfiction, resembling experiences and events the author has experienced personally.

Copyright © 2023 by Syed Haider

All rights reserved. No part of this book may be reproduced or used in any manner without written permission of the copyright owner except for the use of quotations in a book review.

First paperback edition August 2023

Book design by Rameez Mazen

ISBN 978-9948-784-56-2

Haiderthewriter.com

Table of Contents

The Age of Escapism — 5
By The Dining Table — 29
If I Ever Get Around to Living — 48
Acknowledgements — 71

"We look at the world once as children, and the rest through memory."
- Louise Glück

For Melody,

the faint laughter coming through the hallway, and once again, everything is familiar.

The Age of Escapism

The Escapist

i know you dreamt your life would change
but you're in back of the car with your parents again
& the only thing that's gone
is her love from your heart
& the only one that's back
is the hurt
but you know it never left

you've climbed higher
only to fall lower
you've dug a grave bigger than you,
a bit for your body,
a bit more for the boy you couldn't be
& your head's full of memories
of things you never said,
but wish you had the strength

win or lose,
what does it matter
if you're never happy with yourself?
happy or sad,
what does it matter
if you haven't done something good for someone else?
today or tomorrow,
what does it matter
if you never want to be here in the first place?

& any second now,
you'll be looking for the one you thought might be your home
but it's late at night again,
you know no one's coming back
you're all alone in the backseat
& if you fall asleep now
your father won't carry you to your room this time

You Puke What You Inhale

feeling like a deadbeat,
running away from things i created
questions of "is it worth it?"
the sheep are circling over my head
closing my eyes & i'm six years old
picking out marbles from the dirt in my hands

laying myself down in her eyelid,
swinging the hammock
& hoping to slip down to her lips
with her tears

feeling like a father,
they'd all fear to lose me but not
say why they love me

writing a silly poem
on the back of a cheap cigarette box
i know i shouldn't smoke it
but i can't help thinking i'd feel something
puff, puff
crying in my car,
whispering "i'm good enough" backstage
to get myself through the act
hoping the curtains would fall any second
& hope the encore would not come on so soon

Blue Lights

blue in my lungs
from holding my breath around you
blood in my mouth,
from biting my tongue around my mother
& nails deep in my palm,
from clenching my fists around my father

wilted roses in my throat,
from never telling you i loved you
calluses in my feet,
from running after you time & time again
tears in my eyes,
from never taking a blink in case i'd miss you

Sonar

always a "i'm proud of you, haider"
from taking a step further away from me,
& she tells me i ought to be happy with who i've become,
reminding me, "it all finally paid off for you, my love"
but i'm never too proud of what it came at the expense of

ashamed & embarrassed, i bury my head in my pillow
sometimes i'd rather be fourteen again,
than be loved by everyone at nineteen,
too afraid of the cheers & the hugs
i don't know how to make sense of any of it

losing & losing, just to climb somewhere,
anywhere, i don't know where
don't know how to swallow the love,
it's stuck in my throat,
& her name is on the tip of my tongue
i know i shouldn't call her,
but i can't help but wonder if i've made her proud too

Sleep Pretty Darling, Do Not Cry

i wish i was still light enough
for my father to lift me up off the ground
every time i got tired,
& i wish my father was still gentle enough
to carry me in his arms
every time i fell asleep in the backseat of his car

i wish my mother's hair never stopped growing,
so i could get it stuck on my lips
each time i kissed the top of her head

i wish my pillow never swallowed every tear of mine,
i would have wringed them out
just to show you how i felt each night

i wish i never stopped talking to my parents
i kept hoping to hear an apology
even though i had already forgiven them

Time's Up, Grieving's Up!

i carry you over my fingertips
you come out of me whenever i write
& they tell me, "i love this, haider!"
but i never seem to like what comes out of me
mostly 'cause it's you that comes out

i'm tired of hearing that it's been a while & i should move on by now
i did not know my grief came with a time stamp
i wish i could stay on the floor & sink my head into the back of the bathroom door

they'll tell me enough time's spent
but i still haven't found somewhere i can place the love

You Are Wherever Your Thoughts Are

you always fear not being nice enough
always want to look like the bigger guy,
but boy, you're far from being who you wish you could be
& you're not the love you've given
'cause it's not with you & you don't have anything to show for yourself

stop spinning your moral compass
out of hope it'll guide you the right way
you know who you are,
but boy you wish you could be
who you wish you could be

you look the other way,
but you will always hurt the girl you love
it won't get any better, it won't get any easier
you'll only get worse
before you get some help

pretend like she's still your friend
after what you said to her the last time you spoke
you can hide away in your mind,
hoping any day now, love will come knocking at your door

but maybe it's all a dream
i'm having at nineteen
and soon she'll be waking me
kissing my eyes & telling me
"you're only a boy, you can rest

you are running in your mind,
writing all the time
trying to get better than you were

& you are searching for the eyes,
you believe will bring you back to shore,
but they'll never look your way"

Holding Onto Whatever Remains of Us

i get dreams
dreams of the boys we once were
the lives we hoped to live
but we got older,
at least one of us did
but i still get those dreams

i get dreams
dreams of building the house
we promised to turn into a home
for each other,
well, you found yourself another
but i still get those dreams

A Housewife's Diary

i let myself bleed on our bed
in hopes you'd sleep in some warmth
even if you didn't see the color
even if you didn't hold onto me

& i allowed you to cut through my skin
in hopes you'd find a place to rest
even if you chewed through my flesh
even if it was more than i had

i carried the weight of your heart
in hopes you'd finally feel lighter
even if it meant you would fly away instead
even if it was not what i wanted

Between The Four Corners of a Room

when there was no one left
to kiss your head in the morning,
or warm you when you came back home from class,
or hold the *other* hand while you worked,
and when there was no one's arms to drown in,
or eyes to swim in,
or ears to perk up at the sound of your breath
did you still call it "freedom" or abandonment?
when there was no one's heart to reside in,
did you look for shelter or be homeless?

Eternal Reflection

by the blue wall in your room
little lines carved further above
as you grow
till there's no one to carve them

& by your window,
the little boy grows
from wheelbarrows
to grey meadows
his eyes still make you spin

your father's hair grows thin
and his voice weakens
he no longer stands firm
& your mother no longer
looks pretty

& your brothers have moved on
'cause they believe there is something
more to this than being around you
& your little brother has learned
he can figure out the world
without you

& the girl you loved,
has realized you're not enough
nor worth changing for
she's moved on & flown away

A Scar from Me to Stay a Little Longer on You

my entire life has been a vessel for unresolved grief
a vase full of memories
a closed casket with things left unsaid
my arteries stuffed with petals
calluses under my feet from standing still
fingers glued together
i know i should have said something,
i know i should have done something,
but all of me is weak in front of all of you
i've dug nails & clawed on everything i've ever loved
i wonder if you see the indelible marks of me
i wonder if my pain marks you

Restless Farewell

she wrote me a text,
"oh love, i'll be flying in the morning,
this will be our last night together"
it took me a while to text her back,
just in time before she flew away
"oh love, how could you say that?
you'll fly, but not away from me"

she called me from a pay phone at the airport,
"oh flower boy, will you like me to send you
something to remember me by?"
it took me a while to reply,
"oh rosie, how could you say that?
i hold you in my heart, i could never forget you"

she wrote me a letter
"oh baby, i don't know when i'll return to you
again"
i wrote back immediately
"if you must have doubts in you,
if you must call this a farewell,
maybe there is something you could send me,
a piece of the heart you'd reside in next time"

Mr. Misery

you don't deserve to be lonely
but those poems you write
won't make you feel better
pretty soon you'll find
that they're only a mirror
of everything you don't like

i know you feel guilty
but the weight won't get any lighter
stop carrying it all on your shoulders
maybe if you decide to talk it out with her
you'd probably feel better

Book World

you're sitting in the corner aisle
of your favorite bookshop
you always went to as a kid
nobody visits it, you're always there
you read books from start to finish
complete them all there
and put them back in the shelves
you jump from world to worlds
friend to friends
love to lovers
but none of those phrases and metaphors
or those comas or speech marks
would ever embrace you like you pray for
you read a couple of books as a little boy
what could you have possibly known about life
as a little boy?

The Clasp of Hands & Down on Two Knees

i can tell by the look in your eyes
you're looking for a place
to put down your heart
you're just too shy and awkward
'cause you never know
what to do with your hands
here, i'll hold you, while you find your feet
don't trip, it'll be alright

what is my life if not an attempt
to relive the time
my father used to drive me down
to the bookstore
where i'd sit for hours
reading books till the end
losing myself
till he'd call me to check up on me

"how much more do you need to read, boy?
what life will you ever live that way?"
oh well, father, my friend is dead
i don't know who to talk to

You Look Pretty When You Cry

you make me excited
for disappointments
false promises
incomplete sentences
and one arm hugs

you give me butterflies
for heartaches
for throwing up
by overthinking

you make me blush
when i cry
and convince myself it's not true
i pray
you won't think of me
with rue

Onwards & Downwards

my life's passing me by,
but i've only turned nineteen
i'm gathering all the feathers and the pieces
folding my hands
putting them on a little paper boat
watching it go
down the stream of water
i was always afraid to step in myself
but now i have a foot in
i'm tip-toeing in it
hoping i don't lose my balance
'cause i've only turned nineteen

i've been chasing after dreams
gathering up in the clouds
but it always rains when i am near
why does everything fall
whenever i try and hold it?
oh well, mom always said
i was the clumsiest of the three
am i still the same
even at nineteen?

Release

oh dear dead friend,
do you see me now?
i'm flying through the wind
can you see me speaking to you in the dark?
my fists are closing in on the pain
all the memories, all the promises
i'll hold it still
in hopes i find somewhere
to release them

oh dear heavenly father,
do you live through me now?
i've turned out just like you
are you proud or ashamed?
i hold all your work, all your effort
in the palm of my hand
while you held my love
like water between through your fingers
just hold it still
i'll take you somewhere
to release it

oh dear endearing lover,
do you warm me now?
i've been saved by you
are you happy i'm around?
i hold all your pieces, all your love
in the palm of my hand
while you held me in your arms
just hold me still
take me somewhere
you can let go of me

View From Halfway Down

there's a little boy in his little treehouse
laying on the floor
hiding away from his family & friends
& his girlfriend
when they're all asleep
he escapes to his little house
lays on the floor and for hours he weeps

there's a little boy holding his little head
sitting on the floor, thinking of his dad
wondering why he has to become like him
but when they're together
he doesn't look him in the eyes

there's a little boy tapping his little feet
he doesn't know what to expect
he expects bad news
perhaps a slap or a word
they'd hurt the same, he thinks

there's a little boy looking down,
falling from his little treehouse
from the view halfway down
he's thinking of himself
for once and for all
he thinks when he reaches the ground
it'll all go away,
he believes it'll get better
with faith in his heart, the little boy takes the big jump

The Mourning After

been thinking about him for a while now
but i'm too ashamed of what i've done
wonder if he'll be proud of me
does that boy ever think of me?
is this who he wanted me to be?
but i watch him leave through the door
he made a run to the park
right across from the street
i wish he stayed there
digging marbles in dirt
his precious little jewels
with his precious little hands
but i watch him fade away
to the back of my mind
i don't know if he'll recognize my voice
when i call his line
tell him i haven't been fine
his happy time is almost up

even though we barely know each other
i'm embarrassed of myself
and i'm afraid of what he'd see
if he sees
and although he doesn't know me
it still hurts to think of what he might see
if he sees
maybe it's better this way
lonely and away, he fades away
to a happier place

Choking on Flowers

would it be too much
to strip me off my masculinity
to strip me off of what i haven't done yet
to forget who i cannot be
& to find a reason to still love me?

would it be too much
to lower down my defenses
to close my eyes
to let go of the wilted roses
& find a way to hold me?

& would it be too much
to stay?
to be here with me
when you could be anywhere else
would it be too much
if i were to ask for some of your love?
would i be too much?

If You Don't Peak Now, You'll Never Grow

holding my face in the palm of my hands,
while lying flat on a bed full of wasted dreams
& broken promises
a pillow full of drenched memories
& the taste of someone's name
that's still wet on my tongue

if i don't get it right while still so young,
will i ever feel like i haven't done any wrong?
if i keep my mouth shut
could i still swallow the flowers?

i'm not good for love poems
& i'm no good for my mother
i'm not good for sad poems
& i'm no good for my father
i'm not good for anything
& i'm no good for her
i'm not good for anyone
& i'm no good for me

By The Dining Table

Show Me Your Love, Why Don't You?

'i know, i know, but this time's different,'
'& you say that because?'
'well, i'm writing a lot about her,'
'& do you like her or the version of her you created in your poems, haider?'

she was part of all the lyrics
i had my part in the band
we all wrote & sung about her
but everyone kept asking
"who is this unnamed lover?"
and i'd laugh and scratch the back of my neck
hoping i'd summon her arms around me

i was afraid to name her,
once spoken, i could never take it back
i could never shut up about her

she was part of all the melodies i composed,
but there was something about the way she plucked the strings of my heart,
that i could never seem to orchestrate

& i was afraid to name her,
once spoken, i could never take it back
i could never shut up about her

Continuum

i've fallen for a girl
her hair sticks to my lips every time i get close to her
& she sings to me songs i haven't heard of, she draws lines on my hands,
and pretends to know what's in my future

all the while i live in my head & wait to find if this will last forever,
all the while i live in my head & wonder if this could last any further,
all the while i live in my head & hope it could last a little longer

if it were to end,
i would wish to find something to lay my head on when i hit the ground,
constellations splattered over her eyes,
i'm always the first one to look away even after all this time

all the while i live in my head & wait to find if this will last forever,
all the while i hold her hand & pray it doesn't get cold anytime soon,
all the while i keep her in my heart & hope she would stay a little longer

From The Room of Our Cottage House

scooping the crescent of the moon,
letting it hang from your eyelids
close my eyes, fantasize,
about the time i dreamt
of us lying in a garden
we planted for one another,
and our fingers dance over each other
and your lips, so full of love
i still blush when i think of how i could never have you enough

& the berries and the flowers we carry back to our house,
you wash me the fruits
& i place the tulips in the vase
you walk over to smell the flowers,
& i peel you clementines
you paint me a portrait of us
& i write you poetry
neither of us needs to look over the other
to remember the way our faces crescent the two halves of the moon

Kids Falling in Love

i've been finding it hard to say i'm falling for you,
i can't build up the courage
not when you look at me with those eyes
i'm too shy to say it
it's like keeping a bird in my mouth
that chips away at my tooth
i bite my tongue, but it's you that bleeds out

i'd hope you'll be the first one to break the silence,
& then i'll question if i'm a man enough
if i don't say it to you already
i know we're both hesitant about it
we're still haunted by what happened to us
the last time we opened a window into our hearts for someone

but i'd rather let the flowers i picked for you rest by the open window,
so the sun can shine & they can bloom
instead of hoping the light finds a way through my home from some unknown crack,
i forgot to piece together before i fell for you

Echoes of Silence

beautiful as the wind, your hair flies back like dandelions
between the silence,
our shoulders meet
& my eyes embrace your grace
your face rests on my arm when i drive
& my lips crack open to breathe you
while you hold your breath to keep me
our fingers rise on our lap and then fall back

too shy to say it, too afraid to admit it
you'd rather let the strands of your hair stick to my cheek
than to admit you feel it too
but i'd rather write you poems & read it aloud in front of the world
than to tell you,
"i feel it too"

When I Need to Remember Your Face

in my head,
we're standing by your kitchen,
you're grilling me a sandwich
& your mom's telling me what a sweet boy i am,
i'm scratching the back of my neck 'cause i don't know how to react
in between smiles and laughs, our eyes glance from across the room,
you tilt your head & scrunch your nose,
i sink my eyes & smile at you
you slice the sandwich in half & say,
"one for me, one for you"
i take a bite off it & close my eyes,
laughing at how good it tastes
you make a cheesy joke about how you made it with love
& i believe you as always

The Moment That Holds Us Together

we're sitting on the kitchen floor,
laughing & drinking
as i eat from the plate that holds the cake
you baked
you're telling me a story about how your parents met,
while i'm stroking our cat on my lap

your mouth is red from the wine
& your lipstick has stained the edge of my glass
i fight the urge to lean over and taste you
with a mouthful of the cake you baked

the sun is beginning to set
& it melts through our window
to catch a final glimpse of us for the day
but all it ever really does is find some corner in your eye to rest in
while i, as always, watch you with love

Pretend The Mirrorball is Our Mistletoe

walk me to the car one more time,
we'd bump into each other on the sidewalk
i'll fight the urge to ask you, "we should do this again sometime,"
& your shoulder would brush into me
the look of love in your eyes will glimmer
under the moon, i'll be hoping i've parked a little further
just a way to spend some more time with you

leaning against my car, i'm folding my arms,
you're opening yours
& i'm fixing my hair,
while you're twirling yours
i know i should open the door & ask if you'd like to come in
i'm biting my tongue,
while you're opening your mouth to say something,
& my heart's knocking on my ribs
begging me to let it come out
& jump onto your lips
but we can hear the faint music in the back
& you need to return to the party
you're getting emotional
& i'm pretending to look away
a warm embrace once more,
your breath on the crook of my neck
you walk back to the music
i get back in my car

Moon Sparks

we're sitting by your kitchen table
it's cold outside,
& you've made me coffee to warm my hands,
the wind's howling against the window
& i'm imagining how my fingers would flow through your hair

you're smiling at me in the vacant parking lot,
but the moon's right above you
& i'm in awe of how the crescent takes the shape of your eyelids
i know i'd write you another poem some day
& i know you would say "it's nice" as usual
but you'll never see
it's all for you,
all 'cause of you
all about you

Sweet

& something inside of me says,
"go back home,
back home to the woman
that taught you how to love"

& something inside of me tells me,
she's waiting by the kitchen
peeling oranges for me,
for when i return

& something inside of me remembers,
the flowers in her hair flowing over my eyes,
every time the golden slumber would rise over the horizon,
& set in her eyes

Wherever You May Be

when i write you poems
late at night
i wonder where you are
and if we lay
under the same moonlight

when i sing you these chords
by the sunrise
i wonder where your heart is
and if i am still plucking it

when i kiss your eyes
by the sunlight
i wonder where your gaze is
and if i'm still
at the center of it

I'd Wear a Dress or Two for You

inside your house
your arms around me feel like pieces of the moon on my skin
my eyes haven't opened themselves
since you've left my gaze
they refuse to look at anything else
and my lips haven't opened
since you kissed them
they refuse to talk about anything else
and my hands haven't stopped shaking
since you last held them
they refuse to hold onto anything else
and my heart hasn't beaten
since it let you go
it refuses to house anyone else

outside your house
in my car, where i write this poem
on the plastic bag
wrapped around your flowers
i'm trying to make my handwriting look pretty
so you can feel how precious it was
that you held onto the tulips i promised

i hope your parents like me
when they see your smile
and the rose tinted cheeks
as if they were rubbed with petals
i hope your parents like me

Behind The Closed Windows

in the morning, when we awake,
our bodies wrapped in blankets
your hair on my face,
and my arms sinking into your ribs
i don't ever wish to be apart from you

your fingers tapping on my lips
as i kiss each one of them
& your bare stomach pressed against me
your leg over my waist,
you're glistening over my eyelids

& your upper lip
is carved into a crescent of the moon,
your mascara is rubbed off into the edges
of your pillow

you brush your hair off my face,
placing your lips on mine,
and my lungs breathe you in until they go blue,
& i feel the sunshine over me
but the curtains are drawn
i know it's you,
i know it's a good morning

An Open Letter

my fingers miss your gentle kiss
how they'd press against you and never let go
how they cried, they loved
how they vented, they feared
how they confided, they rested

my heart misses your warm embrace
your graceful eyes when you'll let me in
no matter what time or what day
always some space
somewhere in between
a coma or an apostrophe
save some space,
for me

To Whom It May Concern

you're the prettiest boy i've seen,
i'm too shy to say it,
but i need you to know i'm praying
you'd ask me to smell your hair any second

& you're the prettiest boy i've held,
not that there's a long list anyway,
but i need you to know i'm hoping
you don't see the look in my eyes when you're writing about me

& you're the prettiest boy i've kissed,
too happy to admit it,
but i need you to know i'm wondering
if you could feel the same way about me
when we're together

& you're the prettiest boy i've adored,
can't believe you're mine,
but i need you to know you're stealing my heartbeats
everytime you touch me

Waltz For Rosie

got all twirled in your curls
caught swirls in your eyes,
oh i've always been a fool,
in love once again,
i don't even fight it
i won't even remind myself of last time

wrote you a poem on a napkin,
and a song with no melody,
confessed my feelings for you in my head,
but i was shy, so i swallowed it all

dreams of one last kiss still linger,
i wonder if she still remembers
the promises made under the sunlight,
meant to be fulfilled in the arms of the moon river

wrote you a letter on a napkin,
and typed out a stupid paragraph in my notes,
confessed my feelings for you in my head,
but i was shy, so i drowned in it all

Don't Fly Away, My Beautiful Bird

it's been years,
& i wonder if i can still be the same boy
you once loved,
but i know i missed that train
because i was still thinking about the one i got off from

& i know you've flown in someone else's sky ever since,
but i still looked out my window all this time,
hoping you'd once again appear,
hoping you'd once again fly over here

i know we've changed,
& the tides of life have thrown us aside
but i'm still waiting to find you by the shore
when i swim my way back to you

Rose Colored Girl

maybe you're not as pretty as i've made you sound,
wrapped in my metaphors & phrases,
laying between my commas & apostrophes,
perhaps you're just someone else
i've mistaken for poetry

& it would be cocky of me to admit,
you had only given me things to write about,
served me as some kind of muse,
till i realized i only used you
to talk about someone new

did i ever care that much?
is there anything more for me to write?
you've shown me all your shades
there are no more colors to you
you've bled yourself out dry
there's nothing more to you i can ink my fingers in

with the passing of each howling wind,
the touch of you fades away
so i search to find the night
i must have thought,
there might be something about you to love,

but i return home with bleeding nails
once again, i had dug too deep
just to find nothingness
at the bottom of someone else

If I Ever Get Around to Living

Long Way to Home

i'm driving back from my best friend's grave,
in the rearview, the silhouette of the one who left me at the altar appears

i've dropped off the girl i have a crush on,
i didn't tell her how i felt either

the scent of my friends has rubbed off the car seats,
& i've closed the windows so they can linger around me a little longer

my parents have stopped calling me,
& my brothers and i no longer speak,
in front of me's a T-junction,
& i don't know which way to go

my makeup has smothered over my eyes & cheeks
summer's full moon hangs above me,
spinning like a mirrorball
& i don't remember which way's home

on the news,
there's been another bombing,
somewhere not too far from where my grandparents live
& on my phone,
there's another email,
from my professors reminding me to submit my paper on time

despite all the rain,
i'd hope the flowers would finally get to grow

Inside Your Mind

i know it's probably nothing,
& you must've meant it when you said, "i'm okay"
i know i should probably let go of it
but i can't seem to shake myself off it
i know i could have said something better
to ease the pain once again,
& i'm afraid even when i don't look
the blood will still be there

i could have been more
i could have tried to fit in whatever box you needed me to
i could have cut myself a little more to feed you
& maybe if i could have been
what you needed me to be
perhaps i could have stitched you together

but i'm no medicine,
i'm no pill to swallow,
i'm no remedy and i'm no sweet lullaby,
i'm not the kiss over where it hurts,
i'm the wound,
i am your wound

What Might've Been Lost

i know i'll never be that kid again,
i'll no longer worry about forgetting
where i hid the marbles that i stole from my mother's decoration pot
& i won't worry about my imaginary friends going to sleep
without me wishing them goodnight
i won't worry about spilling ink on my white t-shirt

no, no, no
i'll no longer be that kid again,
i'll only worry about if i may lose the strength to get through the day today,
i'll only worry about if i may disappoint my father time & time again
& i'll only worry about if my friends like me or not,
i'll only worry about not being enough

i'll never be that kid again,
i've buried him & his innocence
i'll never write like him
i'll never love like him for i've given all his love away
i'll never look at the world the same again
for i've seen it once
& it'll forever be a distorted perception from here on out

Writers & Lovers

i've been writing about a girl,
too afraid to name her,
i don't believe in luck,
but she's too good
so full of her, i want to open my mouth & let her out,
but so bitter and so sweet, want to devour her

& my mother's been asking me what i've been performing
but i don't know how to tell her i've been telling the world
how she never apologized for what she did

& my father is looking through me
with the hope of being able to grasp something within me
but i take a few more steps back,
the line grows bigger and bigger between us

i've been trying to remember who i was
& how i used to love
but time keeps stretching out in my head
& it's hard to believe i could still be that boy
i'm afraid all the damage would be for no good
i'd say, "i write to say something," but i know that's not true,
so i'd admit, if i don't write, everything else would feel worse

I Don't Trust Myself With Loving You

i know i shouldn't answer your call,
finding any excuse to reach out to me,
haunt me in my dreams,
any way to say you're sorry
but every time you're around,
you snatch away a piece of me
don't know how you do it,
don't know how you make me flee
away from who i'm trying to be

i wonder what you hope to see
whenever you come around,
do you expect me to open the door
for you, once more?

the blood's all over the floor,
& i'm not there to wipe away the mess
you ask me if i would like to stay a little longer,
& i ask why you still linger
if i've let you go?
but you call me,
just an excuse to not bite on the bitterness
resting on the tip of your tongue
& the self-loathing wrapping your throat
what's all this for?
you rot away in your bed,
i blossom in someone else's eyes

See You Later

i'd say, "i'll call you later,"
just to make myself better
even if you'd never pick up later

i'd write you a letter
just to treat the wound better
even if you'd never unfold the paper

& i'd text you tonight
if i thought you'd wish me "goodnight"
even if i knew you weren't alive

i'd bid you a goodbye
if i felt good about it
even if i knew i'd never see you fly in my sky

In My Head, It's Still April

it's april twenty first,
your birthday,
we're texting each other,
& i'm telling you, "you mean a lot to me"

it's april twenty seventh,
we're sitting together in class,
& i'm reminding you, "hey, man, don't put your science book in my bag, again!"

it's april twenty eighth,
we're hanging out together,
& i'm telling you, "stay a little longer"

it's the morning of april thirtieth,
your mother's crying to me on the phone,
& i'm telling her, "i promise i'll pray for him"

it's the evening of april thirtieth,
the doctor can't look me in the eye,
& i'm begging him, "just one last look, please"

it's the first of may,
& your science book is in my bag
it's all i have left of you

Under The Disguise of The Moon

never meant to text you late at night,
hate finding out from your friends that i make you cry
& i'm afraid to look into the eyes of the girl sitting next to me,
fear she might see me holding pieces of you over my eyelids

i keep hoping you'd take a peak any moment now
i leave a crack open, just in case you change your mind
i try to keep my head high, pretend as if you're not needed

but i keep hoping you'd walk in any moment now
even if just a little glimpse,
a little touch or taste,
just to know that you still look for me
even when you're not supposed to
even when i'm not there

Under The Realm of Whatever That Keeps You Safe

all that you go through when you're nineteen shall pass
& do not be afraid, your love will last
but that boy won't be the only one you hurt

when you lose your way back,
you could always find yourself
at the house i promised to build you
i'll always stay true to my word
that was always the one thing you loved about me

i'll recite a prayer for you
at the holiest of the holiest places
in hopes my god will hear me
& understand what it meant to love you

when you lose your way back,
you could always come rest
at the house i promised to build you
i'll always love you
that was always the one thing you abused
about me

& when i lose my words,
i'll think of you
& the blood will come pouring, gushing and spilling out of me

At The Bottom of The Bottle

i look back on old pictures
trying to find the signs of the time
you no longer saw me as your little boy

but i keep hoping any night you'd call me
out of the blue,
say you're drunk on nostalgia once again
& have forgotten the bad times
& all the shit you've done
& as always, i'd come running to you

but i'll look back on old pictures
trying to find the signs of the time
you wanted to fly away from my arms

& i'll keep waiting to see you in that dress
you promised to wear for me
we'll dance once more under the moon
& pretend it's our mirrorball

& i'll keep looking back on old pictures
trying to find the signs of the time
you no longer wanted to look at me

Even After All This Time

it's been a while,
feels nice to hear from you again
i know that paragraph i sent you late at night around your birthday
still lingers in your mind
i know an apology wouldn't cut it
not that i'd try to offer one anyway

i keep wondering if you still remember anything about me
& if you ever hear echoes of my laugh in your memories
the truth is, i miss who i used to be
i know i'm not that boy anymore
& i'm afraid i'll never be him again

but i'm doing better,
i'm trying out new things
i'm out with some new people
& i write about some new girl
but i can't help but think if this will go away too
i'm tired of saying goodbyes,
it's all an interval between a "hi" & a "see you around"

is this what it's all about?
just letting people in & letting people out?

In Love with My Friends

i'm not in love,
but the other day,
saif sent me a song he thought i'd find some comfort in,
i'm not in love,
but the other day,
juhi painted me a waterfall & said it reminded her of me
& i'm not in love,
but the other day,
hala baked me the warmest-squishiest chocolate cake
& i told her, "i'd only eat a cake if you've made it," with a mouthful of a slice
i'm not in love,
but the other day,
nada showed me a book that made her think of me,
i'm not in love,
but the other day,
leo told me, "i've watched you grow & i'm so proud of what you've become"
i'm not in love,
but the other day,
i saw the full moon & thought of mayar
i'm not in love,
but the other day,
arsal & hamlet sat beside me, poking fun at each other as i laughed the loudest

& i think to myself,
i may not be "in" love,
but that does not mean love is not around me,
& for a while,
life is fulfilling,
i am in love,
it's some place to be

A Slice of Love for Dessert, Please

i know love's real,
not because my parents told me to give it to them,
not because my family says i must have it for god,
not because my brothers are my brothers,

but i know love's real,
not because i saw it on the tv,
not because i read it in a book,
or heard it in a song

but i know love's real,
because my mouth's full of a cake my friend Hala baked,
& i know love's real,
because the waves crashed into my ankles
& the sand sunk my feet to bring me closer to the ground
instead of being carried away

i know love's real,
because it's all i've ever done with everything i've ever touched,
with everything i've ever loved
with everyone i've ever hugged
i know love's real,
because it's melting in my mouth as i speak

This is Nineteen

my best friend's moving away,
she says, "this is nineteen"
i tell her, "i hate it,"
"you'll be twenty soon, you should get used to it," she says
"it never gets easier," i say

i'd much rather be amongst the unknown & long for her scent
than be left alone in a room full of everybody i know
& hold onto the hope that she never meant to leave
that it was just some sick joke
& she'll walk through the door any second now
& i'll feel at home once again
but she's long gone,
the plane has flown
& her hair has blown away in the wind

from a drive of twenty minutes
and a ten-minute detour to the beach
to a fourteen-hour flight
and the endless search of her in everyone i meet

One Last Meal

an empty chair across from me
i've set a plate aside just for you
i keep hearing your laugh in the back of my mind
& i still remember the sound of your smile
i've put on my fancy suit that you liked
i've put on a tie too, just you could grab it once more & kiss me

i am picturing the sound of your heels
clicking on the floor as you're walking towards me,
i keep sniffing the air, in case i can finally smell your perfume

the food is cold, the vinyl is beginning to slow down
the moon is waiting for us by the window
"she's not going to be coming around anymore," the birds say

i'm applying chapstick every couple of minutes,
out of fear my lips would run dry when i see you
maybe you're eating from someone else's plate tonight,
maybe you're feeding a spoon to someone else,
and maybe someone else is wiping your lips with their thumb and tasting you

but my door is slightly open,
the birds are waiting,
the music is on,
the wind is knocking on my window,
asking if you're here already & if it can come crashing in your hair once more

In Search of a Melody

your sister no longer remembers my face
but time & time again,
she asks for my name
& you turn away, ashamed of what the sound of it brings

your mother wonders about us
but time & time again,
you tell her you let it go for the better
& you turn away, ashamed of what the thought of me brings

your friends never found out about me
but time & time again
they ask if you've ever been in love
& you turn away, ashamed of what the question brings

you find yourself by the beach once again,
hoping you'd summon my arms around your chest
with the crashing of waves beneath your feet,
hoping you'd lie your head in my lap
once more, once again

& we unfollow each other from the world,
we turn our heads aside walking past each other,
you put up that smile that i once ached for
& i fight the urge to not look
i put up the arms you once longed to hold
& you fight the urge to not cling onto me

we tell ourselves "it's better this way,"
even though you know everything about me
& i only know so much about you

you tell me, "i'm sorry for what i did to you,"
even though you know time hasn't healed me
i shrug my shoulders & say "it's whatever"

it's been months,
we haven't spoken to each other
i've let go of you for longer than i got to feel you
i'm wondering if you still sleep in my shirt every time you have a nightmare
& you're wondering if i've forgiven you for what you did to me

i ask about your degree,
& you say it's going well

you're about to graduate
& i smile, "that's great! congrats!" i say to you
even though i don't feel so happy hearing it
you say you're about to move out
& i give you a hug, and remind you i'm proud of you
but i'd rather hope you're happy & i don't know a thing about it
than to watch it from the sidelines

so much time has passed,
& i'm wondering if i'll ever be loved again
you're out with new people,
and the slightest bit of change about you,
reminds me, that somehow,
you're capable of living life without me

we're no longer fourteen,
you've found some other boy to fall in love with
& i've found some other girl to write my poems about
but a piece of me lingers in the way you kiss,
& a piece of you hesitates on my fingertips,
every time i write about someone new

i wonder if you're ever ashamed of what you feel when you hear my name
but i hope it never brings you any pain
& you wonder if i ever mention you to my friends
but i hope they'll ask something about you,
just a way to speak of you once again

for all our hurt & pain,
& all the i hate yous
all the glistening & glamor
i'd rather you creep through the door
than to hesitate on the front porch
i'd rather you break through the window
than to stalk me through the grapevine
whatever to get you to come around once more
whatever to assure you, the love will forever stay in me

you can go find another boy to call your lover,
to bring home,
to fuck up once more,
despite all your flaws,
you're still very lovable
despite all your lies,
you were still worth a fight

with apropos to our demise

a parable of my recurring dream
in search of a melody
with closed ears
& an open mouth since we last kissed

wherever i am,
wherever i've been,
i wonder if i've crossed your mind in a while

wherever you are,
whoever you've been with,
i see you getting on with your life
in pictures from afar

i still have our dreams in the back of my mind
& our promises are pouring out from between my clenched fists
i know there's nothing of you i can hold onto
& there's nothing i can cling onto
but you'd still find traces of my nails deep in your arms

i can't remember the sound of you calling out my name
but i still hear your laugh in my mind every now & then
& you may no longer remember my smile when i looked into your eyes
but i hope you always remember my name

don't let us be someone we used to know

One Last Dance Before The Lights Go Out

when the curtains have fallen,
the fools in love have stopped dancing,
& the mirrorball hangs above us,
will you hold my hand one last time
and dance with me before the lights go out?

between the crowds & the cheers,
when they all tell me "i love you, haider"
will you remind them of what it meant to love me?
will you speak of me with your rose-tinted cheeks
or with thorns around your throat?

when i look up from the stage,
will i find you among the crowd?
or will you be waiting for me backstage?
will you ever make the time to attend my one last show?

when my phone rings,
will i still find myself skipping a heartbeat at the thought of you?
or will i shrug and continue my way?

will you hold my face,
take a glimpse at my lips,
run your fingers through my hair,
& say, "rest, my love, i'll wash it for you"

I'd Love It If We Made It

there's a world waiting for me outside my door
it'll blossom once my feet
touch the floor

underneath my bed,
my "what ifs" haunt me
& all the things i couldn't be

but in her eyes,
i find some place to be
& in her eyes,
i find some place to leave

i'm being me,
so scary yet so thrilling,
i'm carving my way back home
& it all leads me back to my arms

while it all passes me by,
i look up at the sky,
& i may not be there to fly just yet
but the view is not so bad from here

i'm having dinner with my friends,
we're all gathered around the table,
making jokes about some politician
one of them is asking a controversial question,
& i'm quiet, but not because i have nothing to say
but i'd rather admire the smiles on everyone's face

at nineteen,
life's all about eating good food with your friends
& writing poems for the girl you like
through the window, i'm watching the moon crescent my jaw,
& i'm basking my eyes in the sunset,
i'm learning to be me
so lovely & so worthy

(Encore)

i thought my life would change
but i'm in the driver seat
dropping off my friends once again
& i don't know where i'm headed
but i hope i'll be alright

i keep checking my phone every couple of seconds,
to see if the girl i like has thought of me,
but my phone remains dim in my pocket & her face stays lit in my mind

& my head's full of false memories,
of things i can't tell whether i said
or if they were just imagined in my head

am i only me through my poetry?
will i ever unveil the wounds over me?
i'll always think of dying
before i imagine falling in love
my crippling fear of not having done enough

& i hardly ever have the courage to speak
there's only so much i can write
until i chew on my tongue & bleed
all alone behind the wheel,
no more walks to the car,
& no more "we should do this again sometime"

it's me & myself, somehow that's okay
somehow i feel alright
for all that i've loved
it'll always be burned into my skin
& for all the ones i've loved
they'll always be warm in my bones
& for whatever that has left me
will forever live in my heart

Acknowledgements

It's moments like these that remind me that I would hardly have the courage to be doing this if it wasn't for the people who have loved me and been by my side.
      First and foremost, I would like to thank my parents, for being my first ever pillar of support and strength.

I would like to further extend my gratitude to my friends. To Saif, Hamlet, Arsal, Yousef, and Arian – my boys who've always supported me unconditionally.

To Leo, for showing me endless love. I hope I never let you down. Thank you for always being there.

To Mayar, for always believing in my work and helping me edit this book – thank you for reading me between the lines.

To Juhi, for being the kindest to me and Nada, for cheering me on, always.

To Hala, for making me associate anything sweet with her and her baked goods.

I'll also like to thank Phoebe Bridgers for writing, "Scott Street" for I have spent countless nights listening to that song on repeat – also where I got the inspiration for this book's title.

To Suha, and the entire team at Lunar Inn, who've always shown my work so much love. But especially Suha, for gifting me a platform to express my passion and love.

I would also like to give my affection to my best friend, Rameez, who did the cover art for this book, and without her, I'm convinced people wouldn't be bothered to pick up my book. Thank you, Meez, for saying "Yes" when I asked you. I would have not wanted anyone else to do it. Only you could have visualized my feelings. I'm convinced I would have not been able to put out this book had it not been for your love and support. This book exists because you were lovely enough to make me believe I might have done something good.

I wrote this book because I hoped maybe it was time to help comfort someone else just as much as I've been able to comfort myself by writing about all this. It's been a long time coming and writing this "acknowledgment" feels like a fever dream, because I keep pinching myself to wake myself up, but it is real. This is happening. This is real.

Growing up is not easy. It's also inevitable. Sometimes it feels like my life is happening to me and I'm just a spectator, and on other days, it feels like my life is waiting to happen elsewhere, but on some days, I'm living, despite it all.

I'd like to enclose all my love, gratitude, and utmost appreciation to Nagham – my first ever audience and supporter.

I hope this book comforts you, the reader, wherever you may be and whatever you might be experiencing in your life. I hope our attempts to escape cease, and we reunite by the dinner table when we get around to living.

www.ingramcontent.com/pod-product-compliance
Ingram Content Group UK Ltd.
Pitfield, Milton Keynes, MK11 3LW, UK
UKHW042004230426
12048UKWH00009B/539